THE BEAUTY
OF A GRANDMOTHER'S LOVE

The Beauty Of a Grandmother's Love

WRITINGS FILLED WITH AFFECTION AND HAPPY MEMORIES

EDITED BY TINA HACKER

HALLMARK EDITIONS

The publisher wishes to thank those who have given their kind permission to reprint material included in this book. Every effort has been made to give proper acknowledgments. Any omissions or errors are deeply regretted, and the publisher, upon notification, will be pleased to make necessary corrections in subsequent editions.

ACKNOWLEDGMENTS: "Saturday Afternoon at Grandmother's" from *Grandmother's Household Hints* by Helen Lyon Adamson. Copyright © 1963 by Helen Lyon Adamson. Reprinted by permission of the Chilton Book Company and Crown Publishers. Excerpt quoting Frank Field from the article "How Would You Handle It?" edited by Katherine Balfour reprinted with permission from the August 18, 1977, issue of *Family Circle Magazine.* © 1977 The Family Circle, Inc. "Money in the Bank" by Benjamin Spock from the August, 1971, issue of *Redbook Magazine.* Copyright © 1971 by John D. Houston II, Trustee. Reprinted by permission of Robert Lescher Literary Agency. "Grandmothers' Tradition" from *A Book for Grandmothers* by Ruth Goode. Copyright © 1976 by Ruth Goode. Reprinted with permission of Macmillan Publishing Co., Inc. and Curtis Brown, Ltd. "Quotes" by Don Manker from the February, 1971, issue of *Good Housekeeping Magazine.* © 1971 by the Hearst Corporation. Reprinted by permission of the author. "Forged by Time" by Willie Morris from the October, 1974, issue of *Reader's Digest.* Reprinted by permission of the author. Excerpt by Elva Anson from the August, 1975, issue of *Retirement Living Magazine.* © 1975 by Retirement Living Publishing Co. All rights reserved. "Out of the Mouths of Babes" from an article by Roger Turner in the December, 1976, issue of *Retirement Living Magazine.* © 1976 by Retirement Living Publishing Co. All rights reserved. "My Grandchildren Do Not Believe Me" by Marie Harrison Woods from *Good Old Days.* Reprinted by permission of the author. "Grandmother's House" by Mildred Bigsby from the May, 1976, issue of *Sunshine Magazine.* Reprinted by permission of the author. "Small Boy Running" by Mary Louise Cheatham from the *Christian Science Monitor.* Reprinted by permission of the author. "Grandmothers" by Maureen Cannon from *Ladies' Home Journal.* © 1972 by Maureen Cannon. Reprinted by permission of the author. "Meet My Grandmother" from *My Heart Belongs* by Mary Martin. © 1976 by Mary Martin Halliday. Reprinted by permission of William Morrow & Company and W. H. Allen & Co., Ltd.

PHOTOGRAPHS: Jim Cozad, page 32; Richard Fanolio, pages 13, 16, 40, 45; Farrell Grehan (Photo Researchers), page 8; Kathe Hamilton, page 24; Nancy Matthews, title page, page 5; Jane McClelland, page 29; Sue Morey, cover; Bob Segura, page 24.

The Beauty
Of a Grandmother's Love

THERE'S BEAUTY IN A GRANDMOTHER'S LOVE

Like flowers in the window
make a very lovely sight,
Like sunshine after rain clouds
makes the world so warm and bright,
Like lilting flights of butterflies
bring pleasure and delight…
There's beauty
          in a grandmother's special love.

Like melodies of songbirds
fill the springtime skies of blue,
Like each dawn is reflected
in the fields of sparkling dew,
Like soft, caressing breezes
make the world seem fresh and new…
There's beauty
          in a grandmother's special love.

ANNE PARKER

Grandmothers' Tradition

Grandmothers have had their place in every known human culture since history began. In American Indian legend it was often the grandmother who reared the epic hero, gave him his weapons, taught him the arts he then taught to his people — like Hiawatha's grandmother, Nokomis. Today, in a very changed world, Indian grandmothers still teach their people's traditions to their grandchildren.

Grandmothers have sometimes been domineering and powerful, as in the traditional Chinese family. I have watched Chinese grandmothers watching their grandchildren in a New York City playground, looking strangely modern in their traditional black trousers and pajamalike tops. The tradition they keep alive seems to me a humane and gentle one. Power is not, or at least need not be, one of our aspirations today. But wisdom and gentleness surely are.

RUTH GOODE

Children Do Not Realize

Children do not realize
How deep is grandmother love, how wise—
They do not fully understand
The goodness of her guiding hand,
For children cannot even start
To know the warmth in a grandmother's heart,
The things she's done for them alone,
The good example she has shown.
And so they may not always say
How much she means from day to day,
And yet she's always held above
The childhood things that children love.
And as they grow the long years through
That love for her keeps growing, too,
Until they learn the full extent
Of what a grandmother's love has meant.

AUTHOR UNKNOWN

To hear the whispered voice
    of another's heart
      and understand unspoken words
        are talents of those lucky few —
people who are precious to the world.

TINA HACKER

You do not have to
    live close to *be* close.
Loving, thoughtful, imaginative
    grandparents really live
in the hearts of their grandchildren.

ELVA ANSON

There are persons so radiant, so genial,
    so kind, so pleasure-bearing,
      that you instinctively feel
in their presence that they do you good,
    whose coming into a room is like
      the bringing of a lamp there.

HENRY WARD BEECHER

Among my most vivid childhood recollections are my Saturday afternoon visits to Grandmother Lyon's kitchen. It was a huge room that ran along the entire first floor rear of her somber red-brick house that stood in spacious grounds on Boston's Woodbine Street ….

The kitchen was particularly cheerful during the late hours of a winter afternoon when the pale rays of the sun stole in like long fingers seeking warmth from the great old brick oven. The latter, together with a less ancient but still venerable kitchen range — a massive dreadnought named "Leamington" which my Uncle Simon had sailed home from England decades before aboard his clipper ship — occupied the whole spread of one of the room's four walls.

Saturday was always baking day and, even to this very hour, I can conjure up the rich, aromatic smells of brown bread, beans, apples, and ginger cookies baking in the brick oven. It was an old-fashioned Boston Saturday supper, baked in an old-fashioned way by an old-fashioned cook. Bread was always baked Saturday mornings and the highlight of my arrival was the end crust of a fragrant, newly baked loaf of wheat bread, spread thick with butter and topped by a mound of brown sugar. Yum-yum — and you can say that again!

HELEN LYON ADAMSON

Quotes

Grandmother made the "lightest" bread
And the "best" chokecherry wine;
And Grandmother's hair was "Titian" red —
Not "carroty" like mine.
Grandmother had a "piquant" face,
And Grandfather says (I quote),
Grandmother moved with "clipper" grace —
While I — just miss the boat.

Grandmother had no faults at all
(Quote), though it's plain to see
From Grandmother's portrait on the wall
That she looked just like me…
But Grandfather (quote) was simply "doting,"
So Grandmother's quotes, in part,
May be Grandfather simply quoting
From his heart.

DON MANKER

Forged by Time

[My grandmother] was the repository of vanished times for me. Although she would not have understood had I told her, she helped me to have feeling for the few things that matter. I was nourished in the echoes of her laughter. She was my mainstay, my strength and salvation. She was my favorite human being.

When I was a boy, she and I took long walks around town in the gold summer dusk, out to the cemetery or miles and miles to the Old Ladies' Home, talking in torrents between the long silences. All about us were forests of crape myrtles and old houses faintly ruined. Widow ladies and spinsters sat on the galleries of the dark houses cooling themselves with paper fans, and we greeted each lady by turn, and then she told me who they were and what had happened to their people. We must have been an unlikely pair on those long-ago journeys, she in her flowing dress and straw hat, I barefoot in a T-shirt and blue jeans, with a sailor's cap on my head, separated by our 60 years. Only when I grew older did I comprehend that it was the years between us that made us close; ours was a symbiosis forged by time.

WILLIE MORRIS

Money in the Bank

My grandchildren boast, "I have one grand-father and two grandmothers and three uncles and two aunts and three cousins." All these devoted relatives seem to the child like so much money in the bank, from an emotional point of view....

Grandparents can offer a strong relationship to their grandchildren. Their love and devotion are often as intense as the love and devotion parents give. And because grandparents don't have to feel the responsibility for shaping their grandchildren's characters every minute of the day as parents do, I think they are able to enjoy their grandchildren more. In turn the children are able to enjoy their grandparents. Grandparents usually have more leisure too, so they can translate their devotion into such time-consuming activities as reading aloud, playing house and making excursions to zoos, museums and the beach.

From both theoretical and practical points of view, good grandparents have considerably more to offer than baby sitters with equally sound characters. Grandparents' love

has that glowing, doting and possessive fla-
vor that is exactly what gives children their
special confidence in and love for them.

BENJAMIN SPOCK, M.D.

TIME OF LOVE

Life was filled with special times
when my child was young and small,
times of love and happiness…
My heart has kept them all.

Now life is bringing back those times
in a new and lovely way,
times of love and happiness…
I'm a grandmother today!

AMY CASSIDY

Grandmother's House

Once my grandmother walked these floors,
Cooked in this kitchen, opened these doors,
Cared for her children, laughed, dreamed,
    and sighed,
Loved her husband, kept house with pride.
But nowadays there has been a change.
There's no tank to fill
    on the kitchen range,
No more washing with board and tub,
Not even kerosene lamps to rub.
In fantastic dreams she could not know
Of television and radio.

But on my kitchen windowsill
In winter, flowers bloom there still,
And the house knows laughter
    and love and tears,
For they stay the same
    with the passing years.

MILDRED BIGSBY

An Understanding Grandma

In my grandma's house was a long, slick bannister that ran invitingly down the length of the stairway. Time and time again I was warned that the bannister was "off limits." And time and time again I would ignore the warning and take one more quick ride, always barely stopping short of the large, much-loved vase Grandma kept at the base of the steps.

One day, however, I got going a bit too fast and couldn't stop in time. Over the edge of the bannister I flew, sending Grandma's cherished vase crashing into a million pieces!

Looking at the bits of china lying all about, I knew the vase could never be repaired. I was terrified. How could I have been so careless, so downright bad? My first impulse was to run. And that's exactly what I did! I dove under my bed and prayed that no one would ever find me. There I lay, wallowing in self-pity and remorse, when I noticed a pair of eyes peering in at me. It was Grandma. "Oh, oh," I thought, "it's all over now."

"Come on out of there," she said. "I think we need to talk awhile." I crawled out and she motioned for me to sit down beside her on the bed. With hands folded, I waited for the punishment I knew I deserved. Instead, Grandma smiled sympathetically and took my hand in hers. She said, "You know, I remember when I was your age and was bringing the eggs from the hen house one day. I was swinging the basket every which way when those eggs went flying everywhere. I'll never forget how sorry I was. It was worse than any punishment. And I hid, too, just like you did. So we all make mistakes. Even grandmas. All we can do is be more careful next time. I think you've learned your lesson today."

I'll never forget how relieved and grateful I was that she didn't think I was an awful kid. And now, whenever I see others making mistakes, I try to be patient like her. And I'll tell you something, it sure makes life pass a lot more pleasantly — for everyone.

NAN ROLOFF

A Grandma's Gifts

She has the heart
that cares so completely.
She has the hands
that do things so sweetly.
She has the wisdom
that families treasure.
She has the smile
that brings so much pleasure.
She has the love
that brings joy beyond measure.

MARJORIE FRANCES AMES

Grandmothers

Grandmothers are
Sort of special, like jars
For your grasshoppers, stars
You make wishes on, bikes,
And a best friend who likes
You, and pencils, and ice
Cream at parties. Mine's nice!

MAUREEN CANNON

Meet My Grandmother

One of Mary Martin's favorite roles is that of Peter in the show Peter Pan. *Here she tells how her grandchildren Timothy and Matthew combined her real life role as grandmother and her stage role as Peter into one!*

Timothy and Matthew...had never seen me in a show, but they knew my records. Matthew knew them so well, at age four, that he corrected me if I missed one single word while singing to them when they went to bed.

Richard and I had taught the boys to call us *vovó* and *vovô*, "grandmother" and "grandfather" in Portuguese, so when a knock came unexpectedly on my bedroom door at six o'clock one morning I wasn't surprised to hear Matthew calling me *vovó*.

"*Vovó*," he said, in one of those deep bass voices some little boys have, "may I bring some friends to meet you?"

Most of my life I have not been an early riser or, shall we say, at my best upon awakening. I was determined to be the world's best *vovó*, however, so I pried my eyes open, cleared my throat, and asked, in one of those deep bass voices some grandmothers have at 6 A.M., "When, darling?"

"Now," said Matthew. "They're here."

In marched a stair-step procession of little boys. None of them had ever laid eyes on me before. I sat up straight as I could, put on my best smile; Matthew graciously extended one arm in my direction and made the introduction:

"Meet my grandmother, Peter Pan."

MY GRANDCHILDREN'S PICTURES

"Just happen to have them with me…"
 This is what I say.
But when you come down to it,
I plan it just that way!

Just happen to have the pictures
 Of my sweet grandchildren here—
I like it when folks say, "He's cute,"
Or, "Isn't she a dear?"

Grandmothers keep these photographs
And show them near and far…
Their pride is understandable—
That's how grandmothers are!

KATHERINE NELSON DAVIS

IT'S YOUR GRANDMA

There are times you need encouragement
in things you try to do,
when a little faith and trust
is all it takes to see you through—
    And often it's your grandma
    who offers that to you.
There are times when it's so nice to know
that others really care,
when you have a special joy
or deep concern you'd like to share—
    And often it's your grandma
    who seems to be right there.
There are times when you have feelings
that you wish you could convey,
feelings much too full of love
for words to ever say—
    And often it's your grandma
    who makes you feel that way.

KAREN RAVN

OUT OF THE MOUTHS OF BABES

*Here are some delightful remarks about grand-
mothers made by elementary school children and
collected by Roger Turner, who teaches the
fourth grade.*

Grandmother is always saying some of the
most adsurb truths.

I know the answer is no when she gives me
a long sigh.

Grandmother's Easter dress was beautiful —
and it even had a hat that rhymed.

When she is staying with me, she makes
me stay indoors until the rain stops. But she
lets me go outside when the mud tightens
up.

I don't like to eat Grandmother's scrambled
eggs when she gets egg bone in them.

The last cake Grandmother baked, I got to
plaster it.

For some reason, children can have twice
as many grandparents as parents. This is
just to know, not to understand.

My Visitor

I have a visitor today
With a lilting laugh and a charming way.
She enters on a cloud of pink.
She's never looked lovelier, I think.
I ask her to sit down awhile
And she gives me a warm and winning smile.
We have refreshments — she likes that —
And then we have a little chat.
She admires my knickknacks on the shelf
And I tell her just to help herself;
She chooses a tiny glass giraffe
Whose neck and long legs make her laugh.
In a little while, she has to go,
But I've enjoyed her company so…
She leaves, and blows a kiss to me —
My favorite grandchild — almost three!

KATHERINE NELSON DAVIS

Just the Same!

When I became a mother,
I thought that nothing else
could ever make me feel
the same again.

But I just became a grandma,
and this smile upon my face
holds all the joy and pride
I felt back then!

DEBRA CROWE

Blessed be the hand that prepares
a pleasure for a child,
for there is no saying
when and where it may bloom forth.

DOUGLAS JERROLD

SMALL BOY RUNNING

The little golden boy
    runs eagerly,
Both arms thrust out
    behind like unused wings,
Blonde, silky hair
    tossed up in feathered tufts,
Small face intense,
    thrust forward, loving things.

The world is WONDERFUL —
    the grass, the sky!
We trail him gladly,
    sharing double joy,
The same bright moments
    our small girl once brought
Restored to us again
    through her small boy!

MARY LOUISE CHEATHAM

Small Girl Growing

She is a giggle,
Surrounded by curl,
Busily growing
Into a girl.
She is a wiggle,
All hug and kiss,
Making you do
What you would rather miss.
She thinks doors and drawers
Should be opened wide,
I tie them, I tape them,
But she gets inside;
I think I'll survive her,
I spoil and I pet her,
And let her do things
That her mother won't let her.

GLADYS MCKEE

A Garden of Roses

Each spring she plants lettuce and carrot seeds in long, neat rows. Tomato plants are tied to stakes and dutifully watered twice a day. Green beans are grown in abundance, enough to fill the dozens of canning jars in the cellar. But roses—in their own special garden, red and lovely, bright in the summer sunlight, each bush a magnificent bouquet—roses are watched and touched and pampered.

Her grandchildren are visiting for the weekend. The two little girls have gone with her to the rose garden, eager to help gather flowers for the dining room table.

Her gloved hand raises a blossom slightly and she sips its fragrance by breathing in softly. The girls imitate her, closing their eyes to taste more fully, smiling from the dizzying pleasure.

She shows them her method for selecting just the right blooms to adorn her home. Their two-handed attempts to make the long blades of the scissors snip the slender stems make her smile.

There is no scolding when Sarah cannot resist plucking petals from a perfectly formed rose, only a short lesson on how the flowers bloom. She is gentle when comforting

Janie after a hidden thorn has pricked the girl's finger and is patient as she demonstrates how the minor tragedy can be prevented in the future.

When the girls interrupt her with questions that only a child's curiosity could conjure, she is happy to answer. "How many roses do you have, Grandma? Do you put perfume on them to make them smell so nice? Do they taste good, too?"

She shares her special world with these welcome little visitors, permitting them to giggle and chatter in her special retreat. As she teaches them about roses, they learn about love.

STEPHEN FINKEN

GRANDPARENTAL ADVICE

Don't pamper the baby,
Don't run to each cry,
Don't rock that new infant
And don't lullaby,
Don't coddle or cuddle,
That's all there is to it!
Don't spoil that sweet child…
Let us grandparents do it!

MARY RITA HURLEY

My Grandchildren Do Not Believe Me

When I tell my grandchildren about some of my friends who were Civil War veterans, they smile condescendingly, and I know that they do not believe that their grandmother could be that old. They do not understand that when I was ten years old there were many Civil War veterans in their sixties. Two of these were "Buffalo Bill" Cody and Dan Winget, publisher and editor of the "Merry War" paper in Clinton, Iowa. My father, Frank Harrison, learned the printers trade under Mr. Winget, and my brother and I spent many hours watching my Dad set type by hand and Mr. Winget operate his old style printing press.

It was our chore to bring our Dad a hot lunch in a little peach basket every day we were not in school. Mr. Winget was a charming old man and often had interesting guests. Quite often the guest was "Buffalo Bill" Cody who was Mr. Winget's boyhood companion....

Bill Cody was a glamorous looking character with shoulder-length white hair and mustache and goatee. He wore a cowboy-style hat and embroidered shirts and deerskin fringed jacket and breeches and gloves. He was the more glamorous because he was

"Mr. Show Business" to us because for thirty years he had been operating a "Wild West" tent show which toured the Midwest. We loved to attend and watch the Cowboys and Indians chase each other in the wild opening parade before the show ….

Less important to my grandchildren is the name D. H. Winget, but he is equally important to my brother and me. Besides being an excellent editor of his day, he was a poet, and author of a few novels, one of which was titled "Buffalo Bill." Shortly after my marriage in 1919, Mr. Winget was attending an editor's meeting in Des Moines, and he and my father became my first dinner guests.

My husband was a railroad man. I had a full time teaching position, and my guests were there when I got home from school. I had set a pretty table before I left in the morning, but otherwise there was no sign of "supper" preparations, and I could feel the polite disappointment of my guests.

I could feel the admiration, too, when a splendid hot dinner was on the table in about ten minutes. You see one of my wedding gifts was a lovely "fireless cooker" and I had learned to use it well. No one nowadays seems to know what a fireless cooker was. It was a well insulated box about 18 inches on all sides with a hinged lid and a deep well in the center. It came equipped with a deep aluminum pan to fit the well, and two soapstone disks to place below and above the pan. The disks were heated very hot on top of the stove, and the food to be prepared would cook slowly all day and be steaming hot and delicious whenever it was time to be served....

I am sad that my grandchildren believe none of this, but their turn will come when they are old enough to tell their grandchildren that they had a grandfather who served in World War I. Maybe I am prejudiced, but some way, I feel that my memories are best.

MARIE HARRISON WOODS

After the Visit

When they left,
    I started putting things
        back into place,
And then I gradually
    resumed
        my normal daily pace.
I washed the cookie jar
    that was so full
        the day before,
Removed the fingerprints
    from my
        refrigerator door.
I put my crystal back
    out on the first shelf
        of the hutch,
Rewound the antique
    music box
        I asked them not to touch.
I sat back and relaxed,
    reflecting on the days
        just passed
And thought that,
    after all,
        it's nice to be alone at last.

But when I spied
   that tiny wadded sock
      beneath the chair,
Oh, how I longed to see
   that sweet grandchild
      who left it there!

MARY ALICE LOBERG

Grandma's love, devotion,
      wisdom and help
made a great difference in our lives.
   She strengthened our family ties,
helped the children toward maturity
            and gave us all
a greater sense of family continuity.

FRANK FIELD

A Happiness Bouquet

The family
   is like a garden,
   with joy
   for all to share,
With tender, growing blossoms
   that thrive on love
   and care,
And when
   the flowers are gathered
   for a very special day,
They make
   a bright and beautiful
   happiness bouquet.

MARY ALICE LOBERG

Grandma's Quilts

Grandma raised her family on a farm in the days when money was scarce and every member of the family contributed to its welfare. Grandpa plowed fields and chopped wood, and all the kids had chores of their own. Grandma, along with keeping a spotless house, baking bread and growing vegetables, made quilts. And what wonderful quilts they were!

The fabric for Grandma's quilts came from every available source. There were, of course, patchwork quilts pieced together from scraps of material left over from garment making. One I recall was made entirely from old coats. It was so heavy you could hardly move once you got under it! Another quilt came from a great collection of neckties. Once she even saved up old stockings to be dyed and woven into a quilt. For someone who was wife, mother and doctor to a family of thirteen, it's amazing she had time to do any quilting at all. Over the course of a lifetime, she must have turned out more than one hundred— all of them beautiful.

As her children grew up, times became more prosperous. The necessity for making her own quilts became less, but Grandma never gave it up. The results of her painstaking work became treasured keepsakes. My gift from Grandma is a very small quilt, just about two feet by three. It fits perfectly in the doll crib which still holds the dolls I played with when I was a little girl. When she gave it to me, I was extremely proud of it. I knew she had made it just for me. Over the years, it has become even more valuable. Each time I look at it, I recall not only the great deal of skill Grandma put into every quilt she made but all the love as well.

DEBRA CROWE

A Little Rag Doll

It's nice to see you playing
with that funny old rag doll.
You pamper and protect her
though she's so worn and small.
It's fun to watch you dress her up
as proper as can be
and sweetly entertain her
with mud pies and water "tea."
And when she has an accident
and gets a scratch or tear,
I'm glad to have you bring her here
for comfort and repair.
I like it when you carry her
to bed with you at night
and fall into a dreamy sleep,
hugging her real tight.
I like it when you talk to her
and say you love her so —
like another girl — your mother —
did not very long ago.

KAREN RAVN

Some people make the world brighter
just by being in it.

MARY DAWSON HUGHES

Set in Janson, a typeface
based on a design by Nicholas Kis c. 1690.
Printed on Hallmark Crown Royale Book paper.
Designed by Eva Szela.